For Fred,
(scholar & takeover man)

Tealeaf Oracles

Maureen Freer

Maureen Freer

Oct -87

A BOOLARONG PUBLICATION

Also by Maureen Freer
  Square Poets (ed.)
  Writers' Guide (ed.)
  Summer Scrapbook (with Michael Noonan)
  A Common Wealth of Words (with Ken Goodwin — in prep.)
  The Day We Saw The Marigolds (Stage Play)

First published in 1982
by Boolarong Publications,
24 Little Edward Street, Spring Hill. Qld. 4000

National Library of Australia

Cataloguing-in-Publication data.

  Freer, Maureen.
    Tealeaf oracles.
    ISBN 0 908175 38 8
    I. Title.
  A821'.3

BOOLARONG PUBLICATIONS.
24 Little Edward Street, Spring Hill. Qld.
Design, reproduction and photo-typesetting by
Press Etching Pty. Ltd., Brisbane.
Printed by James Ferguson Pty. Ltd., Brisbane.
Bound by Podlich Enterprises Pty. Ltd., Brisbane.

Published with the assistance of the Literature Board
of the Australian Council.

ACKNOWLEDGMENTS are made

to *Gerard* for my most loved poems *Mary-Anne, Michael, Genevieve, Alannah, Catherine & Elissa*

also to *The Bulletin, The Age, The Australian, The Sydney Morning Herald, Meanjin Quarterly, Vista, Square Poets, Recent Queensland Poetry, Vision, The Chronicle, The Courier-Mail, Artlook, The Border Issue*
and to the publishers of *Australian Voices* (Penguin), *Downs Voices, Downs Images, Back Creek and Beyond*
and to the Australian Broadcasting Commission.

CONTENTS

Page

Too Late, Too Early 6

OF LOVE, AND THE GAMES WE PLAY

Reflections On Watergate 8, 9
The Speyed Bitch 10
Not The Seven O'Clock News 11
Sprung 12
The Cup 13
Glory Box 14
Monstera 15
Lilith 16
One Man's Lament 17
The Kill 18
T.V. Ringside 19
Noonkanbah 20
The Message 21
Ad Lib 22
Hard Sell 23
One Man's Muse 24

LIFE CYCLE

Turtles at Poyungan 26
Apology For Unborn Children 27, 28
The Despoiler 29
Letters For A Missing Daughter 30, 31, 32, 33
Failed Poet 34
Lost Heroes 35
Successor 36

OF SAWDUST AND CENTIPEDES

	Page
Kooroongarra	38
Grandad	39
Voices	40, 41
Moving	42, 43
Land Of My Days	44, 45
Village	45
The Place	46

SONGS AND SONNETS

Definers	48
Song Of Spiders	49
Sonnet To Artemis	50
The Prize	51
Coup	51
Skeletal	52

SUBURBAN MUM

Tealady	54
Hen In A Boat	55
little dippers	56
Pianola	57
Growing Crystals	58

SHADES

Cabbage Tree Creek	60
Toowong Cemetery	61
The Plot	62, 63
Centripetal	64
Becoming	65
Death Of A Truckie	66, 67
The Catch	68
O For The Eye Of A Fish	68

Too Late, Too Early
for Bruce Dawe

Don't blame me, friend,
if this book's too late
for the 20th century
Poems don't come easy
(blood from a stone
these songs & semaphores)
while children are crying
& customers complaining
With the hard realisation
my output's indexed
to the cost of living
in a sense   of dying
being terminally afflicted
with *Verses Scribendi*
the deadliest malady
under the sun
& having a next-year-maybe
arrangement with God
thought I'd get in early
for 2001

Of love, and the games we play

Reflections On Watergate

First
we bled him
slowly:
tongues   razor sharp
cut where it would not show
(later   aides
drew blood openly
on the floor
of his white house
but he would not confess).

Punches   each word a fist
aimed at internal parts
purpled his skin
ruptured the spleen
left him protesting
injured innocence.
We said, Watergate man
tell us you are corruptible.
He denied everything.

Beating him
at his own game
nailing him
to a televised rack
attributing blame
we stretched the truth
trying to crack
his intestinal fortitude,
rammed down his neck
the rotten evidence.

Fearing him
indestructible, a god
dread symbol of our times,
we taped the mouth
of this manic visionary,
severed his right hand,
put out both eyes
that mirrored our guilt
and the lies of diplomacy.

We had to find the truth.
Usually the eyes have it.
Behind closed doors
we wormed our way
into his skull
  only to find
  ourselves . . .

Buried
what was left of him
alive.

The Speyed Bitch

The speyed bitch
turns round three times
trampling ghosts
in her bed.

Tomarctus the wolf
threatens and prowls
nuzzling her dreams
with his wedge-shaped head.

Saluki the hunter and Aibe,
huge paws upon her,
snarl for possession:
her loins drip red.

She moans, recalls,
then sniffing the wind
turns three times more
that ghosts be laid.

Milk bursts her belly.
She whelps, licks clean
and suckles her young
in phantom sleep, afraid

to waken alone and cold,
no warm cubs slobbering
in her bed, a bitch
liberated, speyed.

Not The Seven O'Clock News

In a country short on faith
strong on cynicism
an appearance of the Blessed Virgin
was hardly news.

The A.B.C., sceptical
since 1974
maintained a scholarly indifference.

The commercial media
hardened by 40-second apparitions
Mr Sheen walking on the furniture
Trix on the water
Retravisions
all those fabulous lemons popping
in supermarkets, the miraculous
cleansing, not to mention
out-of-this-world electrifying performances
by AC/DC, Elton John and Slade —
dismissed it as an unconfirmed sighting.

Meanwhile in the southern capitals, inhabitants
of God's own State, Mal's country
were unsurprised: the supernatural
feats of ministers, wizards juggling
figures, fat cats swearing
oaths and prophecies
Canberra's daily revelations
the signs were there all right
stocks and shares
writing on the wall
the '29 Depression
Fatima 1917
and earlier Lourdes.

Only a few then — humble penitents,
harpies praying for redemption
of Australia, and cripples willing
to be born again — gathered, were seen to nail
a cross on the typical gumtree. Some claimed
to hear her voice, calling clearly
for prayer and repentance. Only that.

Not a news item, really.

Sprung

Above the clack of typewriters
cybernetic computers
secretly
desiring the pert new secretary
with tanned Twiggy legs
and braful of knockers
he takes coffee
and an eyeful of centrefold
wondering
is she really lovable
or just a sex object
fantastic creature

But they know his game
male perving knavery
the Ms opinion-pollsters
from Dull Bright & Co. —
the acid-tongued bookkeeper
straight-laced switch operator
phonetapping, eavesdropping
flirtatious Girl Friday —
they tantalise and titter
an officeful of chairpersons

On his desk at lunchbreak
one of them, a pouting
aggressive women's libber
fresh from the typists' pool
leaves a black lettered sign
Male Chauvinist Pig
Redfaced at two o'clock
when no-one is looking
he files it away
for future reference

The Cup

It will eclipse all Moombas, we will gather
tremulous at Flemington beneath the elms
under the stately poplars near the showgrounds
(eyeing the fillies in the fashion stakes
who stamp and toss their manes in the enclosure)
beside the birdcage, in the betting rings
where owners, trainers, bookies, confidence men
jockey for a close-to-the-rails position
explaining Cup mystique with solemn gesture,
daring to sniff the urine-scented turf
for traces of Tulloch, Arwon, Magnifique.

Aah! We murmur, savoring the legend
of two-mile races run on sweat and guts,
"They're racing!" And they are, past the straight six,
thudding and heaving, handwhipped to perfection,
into the final corridor of splendour
trapped like motes within the shuttered eye
of the camera-god. Our voices thunder,
"HYPERNO FIRST!" But where is Dulcify?

It's always like this. Always we kill our heroes —
Phar Lap and Chifley, Holt Lyons and Curtin —
slay with indifference each straining champion,
put down the horse that falters, should have won.

Glory Box

From the age of twelve
              she kept a glory box
filled with fancyworked linen and laces
doilies, pillowshams, antimacassars
admonished by long-widowed Aunt Emily
on everything a girl should need

At twenty she added
              a pure-silk handkerchief
left in haste by the dashing lad who
pressed his suit one Valentine's day
against the pincushion on Aunt's sofa
              then went away.

At thirty she noticed
              telltale wrinkles
age-marks on the folded finery,
mould on the cotton damask, so she
aired the quilt satinstitched with cupids,
              and the yellowing suppercloth.

At forty gave the lot
              to St. Vincent de Paul —
shams and sheets, runners and samplers —
except the satinstitched quilt now spread
in memory of Aunt's crochet-hooked fingers
              on the four-poster bed.

Forty-two in February
              the meterman entered her
apartment looking for
              faults and found none.
Pinning her hair
              after he'd gone
she smoothed the quilt
              consummately embroidered
then took up the thread
              of her life and needlework.
Struggling for hours
              to recall the intricacies
of point and petit point
              patterns she wondered
what would Aunt Emily think?

Monstera

In Brisbane's backyard, tropic flowers grow
and monsteras invade the patio.

Three years I nurtured it, the monstera,
handsome climber with strange slotted leaves
bearing in Spring the mushroom-coloured sheaves
that yield to pine-shaped fruit. Earthenware
pot could no longer hold it so we made
an indoor garden for the plant to spread.

Our wedding day he'd bought it as a gift
from some green-fingered Greek at Shoppingtown
to the old sprawling house, lawns overgrown
with cobblers' pegs and burr. I treasured it
fruit-plant valentine for future years,
learned to water it with secret tears.

She came last night, his favourite visitor,
Maranta of oval face and brilliant tongue.
Pretending work they frolicked in his den
and clinked cool glasses near the monstera
all unashamed. Waking red-eyed at dawn
I searched the indoor garden, found him gone

but in a chaise-longue, ivory shoulder bared
the beautiful Maranta, clasped in death
by one strong tendril delicately flared
in coils around her throat, and underneath
the disarray of robe, a telltale tit
agape at the indignity of it.

It's morning now. Again they'll probe, enquire
how she was strangled. Beside the latticed screen
philodendron nudges the wintergreen,
primrose nods over the trellis wire.
But in the corner, solemn and undeterred
Monstera gazes, does not say a word.

Lilith

Don't whitewash me. These sins
are black as cows' guts, overwrought
with such a wild intemperance, conceived
in sleek perspiring couches of the soul.

Hear then my pulses drumming,
blood of prolific forbears shouting out
mad phallic reassurances. No flesh
of decent disapproval, curt withdrawal
may hold this raging tiger to the leash.

Improper for a woman
to be frank? Better to take your ease
with such reluctant maidens as pretend
love is a two-faced no-game while they weave
desire in prim hypocrisy's cocoon?

I am a shameless woman, then. Come on.

One Man's Lament

All day she teased with painted warlike eyes
dark silken-lashed and dangling jewelled hair
such as maids from a Minoan frieze
to after-dinner battles wore
or proud Egyptian girls of nubile grace
long necks adorned reluctantly to please
barbaric captors from a Hittite shore.

That night reduced to bare essentials, she
lay willing victim to her foreign lord
stretching each fibre of credulity
from real to unreal conqueror's reward.
Taking the wrappers off, the padded blouse
false eyelashes long wig and underlace
flaunted with cruel intent to defraud
she waited. Tricked, I faced a stranger's face.
Lights out, eyes closed, I gripped her brazen hair
laying a ghost . . . wishing *she* were there.

The Kill
for Mohammed Ali, 1981

Tonight
at Caesar's Palace
a pair of gladiators
mismatched for easy killing.
In the packed arena
fervent women screaming
''Come on, Ali, fight!''
to God's last messenger.

I AM THE GREATEST.

His opponent
does not want to kill him.

Hand in glove
he moves
like a desperate man
covering up
against the ropes
legs gone. The crowd
wants action.

His opponent
knows what is expected
and draws blood.

In vistavision colour
sacrificed, he sees
one god, holy dollar,
blinding both his eyes
gilt-edged prophecies
lure of the promoter:
MAN, YOU ARE THE GREATEST.

His opponent
is crying.

Brethren, let us slay
each champion, smash
every golden idol. Camera
lights flash. As at a funeral
darkly we recognise our own
perdition, savoring the lie
no-one wanted to see him die.

T.V. Ringside

"It's a basic, manly sport", said the
manager of the Colosseum
to a well-heeled promoter
and one ageing vestal virgin
screamed loudmouthed "HIT im, HIT im"
to the sadist lion or Christian
gladiator mis-matched for
benefit of electronic viewer.
"Violence is therapeutic", he said,
"in these more civilised times",
wishing the cold grey screen
would come alive with new dimension
of sweaty ringside smell, saliva,
and rich red blood in the arena.
"Men pitted for strength, releasing
hostilities with bodily contact . . ."

On video disc replay, I saw
the keenest bloodiest amateur
wipe his papier-mache face
grin and say something funny
after the final punishing act
of knockout, miraculous survival.
"It's the honour of being seen",
he said, "on the screen.
                    Not the money."

Noonkanbah

As the drill rig
bored through the earth's crust
        disturbing
        layers of antiquity
        enshrined in rock
the goanna god
sensing a threat
to his interior life
        screamed aeieeeeee
till geologists pondered
about the sound waves
when the oil/gas bubbled.

Today in my garden
        one stony hectare
        of dreamtime suburbia
        transformed with jasmine
        and all my days' labour
there's a ground fault, a seepage
an oil-rich stratigraphic trap
        for the unwary. Rumours
        are rife. Men gather
to picket my fence. They'll soon
grab this site where I've sweated
        thirty years of repayments
        and still not entitled.
Patrolling the patio
and taxed to the limit
I rehearse every line:

        Deep down in my garden
        a spirit is waiting
        to haunt the intruder.
        And guarding the gateway
        this Moreton Bay Fig
        limbs bent like a sorcerer
        is pointing the bone.

Let him who is without gods
lift the first stone!

The Message

He spoke of peace
and the brotherhood of men
said *Blessed are the poor*
Make love not war
They marked what he said
and used it against him.

His followers wrote books.
and slogans of PEACE
in temples and mosques
even in the market place
where sinners were stoned
or regularly drunk.

One day in the Square
someone painted a sign
     Persist
     Enlighten
     Assist
     Cooperate
     Endure
Even the dumb and the blind
seemed to get the message.

A stirry crowd gathered
men scoffed and sneered
tore down the placard
some poor beggard was cured
another wanting to demonstrate
against the law of gravity
climbed the nearest skyscraper
(out of mind, out of sight)
and while ascending into heaven
full of fire, full of grace
hung a Good News placard
indelibly in space:
     Pray
     Everyone
     Acceptance
     Changes
     Everything

Nobody could change that.

Ad Lib

I'd like to come
to where the flavour is
menthol green
sunlight lemon liquid
beans in every cup
push the k.o. button
see the lively bubbles
fly the friendly way
up   up   up

Pure and simple
fancy nancy fancies
it's the real thing
the orange experience
with the black label
new active eight
it may look small
go, little big wheel
fillerup with goldie
and the feeling's great

Is it as good as
the people mixer?
Everybody doesn't like
a white tornado
this is Australia
a little dab'll do
NOBODY CAN LIKE CANBERRA CAN
poor old Louie
said the lemon-charged lady
how could I tell him
I wanted two?

Don't wait to be told
keep on keeping on
put sparkle in your day
join the jigglers
carry the big fresh
pot to the tea
feel twice the cat
get a kick
marlboro country
even satisfies me.

Hard Sell

for Norm

This pantihose all-girl
with silken hair streaming
and long legs running
through fields of fun
glides through my television
and lifts me setwards —
but the action ends there
before it's begun.

*For there are Indians, Indians all over the screen
whooping at settlers crouched in covered wagons
brandishing knives and scalps of burnt-out heroes —
Custer's flaming heroes in every scene.*

That pantihose girl again
with loose hair flowing
and silk legs striding
through acres of corn
throws me one sideglance.
Traps one more viewer.
I rise to join her
breast-heaving fun.

*But there are frontiers, frontiers still to be blazed and crossed
and this pain-in-the-neck of a lawman hard as steel
keeps fighting for justice and the American Way
while I fight to remember her way, her look, her feel.*

At last, a commercial.
But there's no girl showing
smooth thighs and dimples:
the bird is gone.
There's a suave cigarette man
from Benson and Hedges . . .
That pantihose angel
was having me on.

One Man's Muse

Words excite me:
Magazine wants poetry.
Olympia glares
unused, from the corner.
Her metallic eyes mock
this unlikely Homer.
Spring issue, September.
Sensations come bursting
like rays from Apollo.
Thoughts smoulder.
Inspired, I follow
the muse, take Olympia
(portable, she bends
her frame to my needs:
her keys and my fingers
could unlock an illiad).
We make an heroic
couplet together.
One day there'll be odes
and small terza rima
with triplets and sonnets.
But right now she baulks
as my pale flame ignites
stuck fast on a comma.

Dear editor, how slowly
this frail pencil writes . . .

Life cycle

Turtles at Poyungan, Fraser Island

"They're mating", he said. "We're watching
a pair of turtles, mating". (I thought:
surely, porpoises). Grabbing binoculars
he ran, hammer and shed forgotten,
over the clifftop dune, suddenly eager
for facts of life.

Off-shore, brown
below Poyungan, big as kitchen tables
they swam, two Loggerheads dexterously
making love, heedless of waves'
thunderous applause, front-row casuarinas
nodding approval.

And the delighted boy
at fifty years of age, recognising
life's cycle, rapture of sea and turtle,
celebration of earth sky and water —
leaned an arm on his grandchild's shoulder,
holding the moment's joy, horizons of sun
slanting to a blue limitless ocean.

Apology For Unborn Children

APRIL.
No sign. No sign.
Only a month beyond conception:
already the torturers move in.

Another child. At thirty-five
ten more years of proved fertility
gape at my madness. Worldly-wise
women with cycle-calculating eyes,
pills discreetly tucked in bedroom drawers
smile at my naivete. To justify
this extra mouth thrust on a hungry world
is for demographers. I think only
of rough probings, agonies, deliverance.
Somewhere along the meek child-bearing line
defiance grows, the mammal dries. Mind drowns
in seas of sleepless nights, infantile vomitus,
wet beds. Exhausted utterly, I dare to pray:
Lord, from this unplanned child, deliver me!

JULY.
Abortionists with prophylactic knives
carve up my dreams. Nightly in Limbo
half-developed forms parade their innocence,
crying out for names. To be or not to be
forever begs the question of my woe. I rise
to meet them, refusing to pay lip service
to fine creeds. At last, there is a choice . . .

Here's legal tender for death, abortionist!
(Foetuses struggle, born before their time).
Hide them in buckets. They stare, uncomfortably real.
Viable, smother them. Who has the right to exist?

SEPTEMBER.
There's no conscience like a clear conscience,
no beast like a pregnant one kicked hard
in the belly by unborn feet. Mind swells
at this enormity of misery; old wounds throb;
varicosed parts rupture. This is the time
to make good use of suffering, with some offering
to expurgate guilt of yet another
forgotten soul suffering its purgatory.

DECEMBER.
This is the season when ripe mangoes drop
and eager teeth tear at the golden fruit
juice trickling breastwards. Time for deliverance!
Like welcome enemies, the pains advance.

The labour of my nights and days
burns inward to the brain. There is
no other pain like this, no sound
like yell of newborn human bawling air
with navel-cord cut free of the placenta.
There is no other joy like this, the push
of small hands searching, exquisitely curled.
Dumbly I hold the child I did not want
the threat-of-child made flesh of my own flesh
against the urgent breast ungrudging now.
Somewhere within a mind's dim puzzled groping
flickers brief cognisance of a plan —
body to bones, bones to dust, dust into flower
sprouting from some vast eternal tree.
My own loved child, this much I only know:
I am the spent leaf wintering on the bough;
you are the bud that opens as I fall.

Welcome, sweet stranger, to a stranger world.

The Despoiler

There is a permanence about sand castles.
Given a low tide, quiet beach and three helpers
five, eight and ten, you can build malls
administration blocks, freeways, city halls,
even a random-sculpted suburbia
along the beach, and though the south-easter
threatens and scours, still firm it will stand
this new metropolis carved from sand.

Hours pass
like generations. Children paddle.
Gulls circle
the sand-city in formation, observing
the tide that laps increasingly the shore.
Have we built above high-water mark? Thus
towns survive between the tides of war.

But here comes the despoiler, aged two, Elissa,
enemy disguised with sunbonnet, atomic
blue eyes bent on destruction, swift feet
crushing the houses, bridges, offices
to rubble. Hiroshima! Our buildings tumble!
O Elissa
                to think the tide
                                was what we feared!

Letters For A Missing Daughter: Europe Revisited
A poem for voices

Cosne. Good trip. Europe is fantastic.
My room overlooks the Loire — terraces
of tulips, almond, peach. The river road
afloat with fishermen, pink and white blossom,
two mornings weekly, market day, the vendors
cheese, flowers, clothes, farmcooked bread
tea-strainers, cassettes — I love them all.
Henning is here. We argue every day,
write songs and poetry, compose ourselves.
Glad that I left teaching. So far away
it all seems, Michael's December wedding.

Photos herewith. Notice your brother's groomsman
hugging a certain bridesmaid? He says to ask
will you be home for Easter.

April 30. Springtime in Avignon!
It was here we met, three years ago exactly.
Henning is painting a swan, electric blue.
(There was one that day in the gardens, we discussed
its movement like idiots, beauty and form,
throwing centimes into the petalled water
breathless both with spring, myself shy
girl from Oz, unaccustomed traveller
H. persuasive German. Entranced for hours
we spoke in awkward French of lake and swan).
He paints it blue now. Why blue? He says colour
like love is in the eye of the beholder.

August. Got your cards from Lourdes and Bonn.
Pleased his family likes you. A fairytale,
with floodlit castles harbouring the Rhone.
Does *everyone* have Mercedes? Winter here
the usual joke. Cool nights, warm days, frost
only in distant places like the Lockyer.
Busy as usual with the Exhibition.
Rita's pregnant, giving up teaching soon.
Michael's jubilant, to be a father.

September. This picture taken in Assisi.
Intentions for you at Mass. Even Francis
poorest of saints, has a basilica.
Also petitioned Our Lady of miracles
Tuesday at Perugia Cathedral.
*Ever heard of the Virgin's wedding ring?**
I've seen every crypt and palace in Umbria.

December 12. Brisbane's steamy weather
cooks us to perfection. Mango time
in every second backyard, and the fruit
ochre-yellow luscious delectable
clings to our teeth, mango nectar sweet
on everybody's lips. Impossible
to eat politely, so we slurp and wallow
knee-high, languorous in hairy seeds
and papaws left by latenight flying-foxes.
Will you be home for Christmas?

Europe's freezing. Going tomorrow
to Greece. Warmer in Rhodos. Bleak
winds straight off the Alps. Try tugging
a sloshed suitcase through the Venice sleet.

No news for ages. Are you alone? Alive?
Any chance you might be getting married?
We saw the Old Year out — nine of us
family together again, Mooloolaba
flares exploding green/red over the river,
carhorns tooting, campers making a din
with bucket and tincan, singing the New Year in.
We missed you.

Whoever mentioned marriage? Silly question.
None of your business really, anyway.
Living (just)
mainly on cheese and olives.
Money running out, and H. is leaving.
Think I'll go to India via Turkey
(Marmaris), perhaps end up in prison
(joke). Hope to be home some day.

**Perugia Cathedral has what is claimed to be*
the Blessed Virgin's wedding ring.

March. Come home. Bunya nuts in season,
Bopple and Kingaroy. Clem says: ''Best
boil them slow in salty cornbeef water.
Nothing better, Bunya nuts and beer.
And bring a gun, the valley's full of deer.''
That King parrot's back in the same place —
camphorlaurel near your bedroom window.
Sending money, National Bank of Greece.

April. Phoned, they said you'd left. Ages.
Letters and money returned. Please write
advising address, contact the Consulate.

June. You do not write.
I picture you
locked in cold embrace of the Aegean
waveswept past the hostile Sporades
adrift for days, your pale body floating
gold hair streaming water, at Marmaris
washed ashore, another alien
taken by uncomprehending Turks.

But there is news from Athens, a girl tourist
plunged from Mt. Parnassus to her death
still unidentified. Was she searching
for Homer, Hesiod, or her own self?
*Treading the cold slopes, winds of despair
swirling among the ruins. Consulted the oracle
at Delphi. But it gave no answer.*
Wednesday I dreamed that Zeus took a maiden
out of the cold mortuary, bore her up
to a quick-healing shrine, kissed her awake.
She laughed aloud, braided her golden hair
with diamonds and sang of love forever.

It is not the end, never
when he leaves, walks off
muttering some weak apology,
about his work — see you sometime —
and you know he won't, it's over,
cry your heart out, weeks, a year
or longer. They say that God is love
and that we take our lost loves to the grave.
The world is full of things we cannot have.
We go on living.

October, mulberry month, and jacarandas
cast their soft purple nets upon us.
We yield to peace, city a smokescreened haze,
Mt Coot-tha afire with yellow-flowered gum.
Fruit and flower, each in its due season,
parrot and bee, summer somnolence.
Michael and Rita staying, baby James
grandchild, our very first, we kneel together
and search his face with absolute reverence.
I remember my parents' joy. You were their first
grandchild. Two months old. My father
waltzed you in his arms, the pine veranda
creaking delight. One year later the grief,
Mother refusing to know that Bruce was gone.
Eldest. *Her* parents first . . . .
So it goes on.

We sow our words on the wind, silent ciphers
of chaff falling on deaf ears, poetry
manuscripts rot in foreign postalboxes
letters returned ''unknown'' or ''wrong address''
telexes tossed aside at the consulate
where parents stand in queues, searching for children.
A thousand aerograms jigsaw our life's sorrow:
patterns fall into place, we know tonight
no-one will read our messages tomorrow.

I dreamed last night you were well, steering a boat
near Lake Eyre, somewhere on Coopers Creek
to an inland sea, the one explorers searched for
(hid in the centre, they thought, of this continent
under gibbered estuaries of sand
alive with bones of men, spider-flower
and mulga trees inscribed ''Dig to Westward''),
past Sturt's Stony Desert, hard hinterland
of the spirit, to a place of coolness, light
with water cascading, crystal birds singing.
You were serene, and heading for the Source.

Please write.

Failed Poet

There was this failed poet, wild
with imaginings, tuned
to thc call of the butcherbird, fazed
with the song of the spheres.

Nights, she heard paper-moths rattling
dry wings in lightbulb chalices
(and still they come, she thought,
wingtips flapping at the window
mesmerised, oblivious to warning —
all those eager worshippers
desiring the light).

Occasionally, the plover's cry
from along the creek, seemed glad
about something, voicing syllables
of her name. On clear nights,
stars sparkling with frost
shed bright revelation. Spiders
sang litanies
in tents of air. And she rejoiced,
fed triolets to the flame.

By day, six children
devoured her, throttled
her with love. Laid
a thousand posies on her
till she was dead.

Lost Heroes

"I am Sir Francis", he said, not indicating
Drake or Chichester. Along his bed
flotilla of plastic ships, a toy armada
braved the swell of blue blanket and pillow.
"It's rough around Cape Horn", he called, suggesting
his Gypsy Moth might not ride out the storm.

"I am an astronaut". In the white nosecone
of his mosquito net he balanced, perceiving
obliquely the dangers of space travel
knowing perhaps, his frail craft Apollo
was doomed ultimately to burn
in the hot dragon breath of oxygen.

Next day he was a soldier, setting out
small for ten years, knapsack overflowing
with mock grenades. I knew he had to go
as brave men must, defending. Fears veiled
I warned, "Be careful of the tree-house",
dreading the mission that might be his last.

After they brought him in, crumpled and dying
he said, "I found it, Mum", not bothering
to finish the sentence, ever. I wondered
was it a moon rock or sea treasure?
Tears are useless things. I'd seen him die
a thousand times before. It's not easy
to cut cleanly the fond apron strings.

And when friends whispered, "She does not weep:
her motherhood is neutered", I was thinking
who in ten blameless years has been
sailor, astronaut, soldier? Grown men
prove valour becoming one or other
yet my son dared be all of these.
Breaking frontiers, tracking stars or charting seas
men must go forth like little boys, adventuring.
And boys, defying death, go forth like men.

Successor

It seemed simple enough, the second owner
searching for property pegs, with one marker
missing. What was the man like, I wonder
who built this fishing shack, remorseful farmer
who hanged himself in prison, murderer
of his own children? I walk the dunes, measure
recheck each boundary, slyly consider
he might have been dishonest, not caring whether
he cheated, lacking each side a neighbour.
And who was here before him? Some invader
from the mainland, dark-skinned survivor
of many a tribal killing, or just a raider
of eugaries, drinking the island sun? I waver
in my search, carefully stepping over
the middens.

Of sawdust and centipedes

Kooroongarra

I saw Kooroongarra the other day.
Often in dreams I go there, seeking
a farm, a house, a milking-shed.
And the weathered house, I may never find it
though I ride all night down familiar laneways
past Paton's bore and Ezzy's haystack
through creeks bone dry or sometimes flooding
and I search the hilltop Evans country
till there in the distance, clothed in light
of a tree-laced sunset, the old house glistens,
with poddy calves frisking late on clover.
I look through a fence, the gate is locked,
a window changed, the chimney broken
and strangers stroll our front veranda.
The watertank grandfather dug from sandstone
big as a barn, is all filled in.
But my mother's there, I hear her singing
as she pummels dough, the kettle's steaming
and Dad's out fixing somebody's mill.
Maurice laughs as he saddles Brownie
for cattle camped in the Big Shade, Judy
is pushing a swing near the pepperina
Del is pounding the butterchurn
and the others are lost, or walking somewhere
in Number Ten, I will find them later —
this dream, next dream, sometime, never . . .
She's changed, that's not my mother singing
and Dad is gone, the house pulled down.
. . . . I always wish I hadn't come.

Grandad

Grandad
didn't believe in them
lavatories in houses
so he built one up the back
a two-seater
carved from cypress.
Half a mile's walk on a cold night.
And we inherited it.

Those were the days
of sawdust and centipedes
lysol and the deadly redback spider,
scissored squares of last year's *Chronicle*
strung from a nail. Poultices. Castor oil.
Alas the painful remedies of childhood
gone in a flash like the Rawleigh's ointment man
Silver Star starch and Mrs Potts' iron.

1980. We visit Grandad, tethered
like a restless horse at the Veterans' Retreat
to a metal handrail overlooking Brisbane.
He lights his pipe, asks news, examines the sky
for signs of rain, gradually unwinds
tales like strands from an old weathered rope.
We gaze at the distance, carpark turns to paddock
balcony changes to comfortable veranda
dripping with summer grapes. We learn of drought
that killed the prize heifer from Toowoomba,
fires at Mt. Emlyn, floods on the Condamine,
bullocks hauling timber for barn and cowshed,
house and yes! a double-seated privy
way up the back, near the bails, you understand.

A bell rings. Time. We rise, make our excuses
escort him back to bedside chair, close doors,
pretending not to notice the ignominy
of en suite royal doulton dunny.

Voices

Mulberries for Maurice. Beads of purple juice
hung from his bristled chin. Each October
"Not a bad cook, girl", scones and mulberry jam
and twelve riotous children, his and ours,
charging like a paratroupe of monkeys
up the wall to pluck ripe mulberries
out of the mouths of birds. Oh poor Maurice
dead at thirty-five and who remembers
here except October birds returning
punctually with avid sharpened beaks
to peck the reddened fruit, the mulberries.

Nothing for Bruce, only the shattered bloodwood
struck by lightning three years to the day
he leaned against it nursing the twenty-two
that cracked his chest. See there, down the slope
north of our house, the gumtree then the bloodwood
split at the base? Bleeding all night he lay
against the mothering tree. We searched till dark
shivered in bed to hear the dingoes howl
their ritual tenebrae of pain and loss.
Next morning a searcher said, "Your brother's found.
Don't let her look. It was no accident".

Lilies for Fred. The amaryllus bulbs
emerge beside the jasmine bush each year
with ironwilled tenacity, and Fred
(B.F. Evans, died nineteen sixty-two)
walks again in my garden, neatly resurrected,
blue eyes twinkling at his son-in-law
who asks of Kooroongarra cows and drought
and how to plant a crop here, to the south
on five small acres. Long into the night
we speak of pioneers, feeling the strength
of early settlers on the Darling Downs
flow from Fred into our eager veins.
He brings his axe and saw; ten ironbarks
fall as we carve a place to build this house
while Bill behind the hut drinks all our beer.

Hers is the pomegranate. To the farm
and its cruel sunlight Molly Mason went
with jet black curls and fairest flawless skin
to cook, scrub floors, cart water, chop the wood
and there beside her door a pomegranate
planted by Fred's mother, Mary-Anne
(who buried twins near the tree in that same yard)
grew to console her. Oh the harsh winds
and the dry times my mother Molly knew!
But through each drought the pomegranate grew
and here is its seed, here at my Bardon place
with scarlet flowers and gold-red rinded fruit.
At times the tree rustles with Molly's voice:
"When are you going to give us grandchildren?"

Large as life in my garden, relatives
long departed still refusing to die —
brothers, mother and father, ancestors
gently tugging the fabric of memory
until I reach out and touch them — MaryAnne
Twidale wife of B.F. Evans the first
(ex Sussex forester), father of Fred
whose Molly bore him five Australians
of English/Irish/Scottish pedigree.
When Easter bulbs thrust upward through the earth,
mulberries ripen, white cedar puts on its leaf
and west winds stir the Brisbane pomegranate
I listen and speak to family voices, speak
as my children's children soon will speak to me.

Moving

Progressive Developers
are moving Gran's house.
It sits on a trailer
joists sagging, roped down
like a trussed chook, torn creeper
of white Singing Ivy
festooning one door.
In the yard's furthest corner
iron fowl-shed dismantled,
with half ripened chokos
still crowding a vine.
The privy is gone.

What do old kitchens smell like
hauled up on a trailer?
Of hot scone and pickles
preserved plum and woodsmoke
blue odorous bottles
of Gran Evans' Tonic
and ivy-geranium pots
on the veranda?

From her high one-roomed window
she may see it move slowly
past Jindalee Hall
(fourth turn, and no neighbour
to fetch Doctor Matthews —
the old girl transplanted
set down like a cabbage
on new Hospice soil).
In her mind she will see it
grey house on a trailer
adrift like a boat:
front bedroom where Johnny
had croup and his father
died after the War.

She will see it go sailing
through tall foreign suburbs
of concrete and stone
down streets half remembered
from days of her childhood
past old latticed houses
on stilts, caught dreaming
of their time to move on.

This twelfth day of March
I duly record it
Gran's house on a trailer
slow travelling past sunset
green tendrils of ivy
whiteflowered and clinging
to the kitchen door, singing.

Land Of My Days

Beyond that blister of hills swelling to sky —
Domville and Pine Mountain where wild pigs
scattered our saddlehorses in alarm;
across the Mingimarny, meanest creek
ever to flood or stubbornly run dry
as beast and man searched heavenward for rain —
lies Our Selection, my father's father's farm
bought for the price of a sawmill at Punch's Creek
and love of a Twidale girl named Mary-Anne.

Tough they were, the 1880's men
Evans brothers, Albert Jim and Bertie
who hauled the white-pine, cypress, iron bark
for huts and churches, Mabbett-and-Silver houses
all the way from Pittsworth to Further Out.
Bertie Evans had axe, crosscut saw
and leather hands that urged his bullock teams
over gullies and slippery blacksoil plains.
Whenever a river floods, the Condamine
breaks its bank out Brookstead, Yandilla way
I smell once more the sawdust, and the man
who put the "mill" into Millmerran town.

And his son Fred took Molly Mason a bride
to Kooroongarra in nineteen twenty-four.
She was a city girl. The prickly pear
towered above the fences; hordes of cactus
spike-eared monsters luminously green
menaced the road that tunnelled through the pear.
And there were wallabies plundering the wheat
snakes, dingoes, scorpions, with crows
plucking the eyes out of the lambing ewes.
For you Fred Evans, I celebrate defeat
by elements of water wind and fire
and your own courage, how you fought a war
in 1918, again in thirty-nine
and daily on the Kooroongarra farm.

But you are not dead. People like you live on
re-enriching this rich land of my days —
Arthur Ezzy, Sid Paterson, Ken Macqueen,
Whitbreads, Patons, Taylors, Whites, Jones.
Wheels turn, men harvest ripened grain
spilling like lifeblood of the pioneers
into the golden silo of our years.

And you with the sawmill, Bertie — here and there
your white-pine sawdust settles on my hair.

Village

Whoever was there, has gone.
Old friends become strangers
and wordlessly move on.
Who cares about changes?

The old house with pine beams
and no running water.
The hayshed, the wheat barn
that harvested laughter.

The quaint school with one room
and six classes in it.
The tin hall, the spired church
with grave faces round it.

General store, burned down.
Cheese factory, banished.
Who cares? *I* care
for friends that have vanished.

The Place

I took my money to the man
with property to sell.
Have you, I said, a cypress house
on a western hill?

With old veranda, knotted beams,
doors of coloured glass
chimney for a fuel stove
and fireplace?

Cypress is coming back, he said.
I've one in knotty pine
beyond the suburbs, just restored
by friends of mine.

Has it, I said, a tower of gates
to keep the brumbies out?
A hayshed and solid barn
to beat the drought?

It must have creeks a waterhole
billabong a spring
that swells to riverburst of frogs
chorusing.

Is there a thickset Evans man
with fire in his veins
furrowing till wheat runs gold
through his hands?

Does his wife still bake the bread
singing in the dawn?
And all their six little ones —
have they gone?

About this house, I said . . . but he
did not seem to hear
with other buyers clamouring
for brick veneer.

Songs and sonnets

Definers
patior ergo sum

Shark's fin and iceberg tip
define, explain
hidden terror's longitudes,
the sharp peripheries of pain.

Dorsal stars that fin the night
signal the lie:
"Believe only what you see"
to Thomases who scan the sky.

And though I prick the fathomed dark
with twin radar eyes,
I feel the crush of ice and shark
as red titanic bubbles rise . . .

Song Of Spiders

All night, outside my window, three orb-weavers
captured in separate air-loomed tracery
fly by night prisoners, moth-shaped unbelievers
who thought that web was air, geometry
of upper space concealing traps of terror
slung in subtle silk, housetop to tree
wheelspoked to mark the paths of error
by spinnarets in tireless harmony.

This morning I see the three space-dwellers kneeling
each in the centre of his universe,
rays of sun like the Holy Ghost revealing
lines more deft than ever spun in verse.
If I could copy their wild harmonies
of shape whenever halting words begin!
Spiders nightly in silent litanies
praise their Maker as they prey and spin.

Sonnet To Artemis

The moon, full-bosomed, white and prosperous
risen from the east in broad daylight
tells her secrets to the startled night,
undoes her golden zipper, generous
in laying riches on the shadowed grass —
twigs of filigree, leaf-coins minted bright,
limbs of trees that quickened at the sight
of her new opulence, bold as polished brass.

Monthly she plays tricks, creates illusions
of wealth and fulsome beauty — hers will fade
even as ours, daily from this night on.
Still we would have her come, feed our delusions
with counterfeit coins, fake medallions made
from leaves that shine as silver, and are gone.

The Prize
(for a race at Gladstone)

Whether he wished to race
was unimportant. Barrackers
making political mileage of his case
pushed, lobbied, laughed and jeered him on.
(I have seen turtles, frogs and party-men
comically vie for similar disgrace
elected unwittingly to high offices).
And so he ran, disjointedly at first,
long pale legs spread crablike, wide,
clawing his way as from a prison camp —
guards who prodded savagely were the worst —
sensing freedom ahead, the salty tide
lapping the yachts at anchor near the ramp.

Luckier the others who were beaten.
The winning crab was clapped, cooked and eaten.

Coup

I'd never have suspected it. This yellow
aggressive leaning Cassia that crowds
my autumn doorway was a spindly fellow
in February, not a sign of buds
that will explode like rocket shells tomorrow.
Today against the greening pane he gloats
over captured territory and my sorrow
at last night's sudden victory, his troop's
invasion as the Ides of March expired,
storming the flowerless bastion of my window —
and not a single scented shot was fired.

Skeletal
for Paul Grano

Gather them, carry them away silently
to the island of broken bones.
High on the driftpile of displaced vertebrae
unbending attitudes, thwarted proposals,
errors, crippled dreams and calluses —
leave your used skeletons.
Heap them along with the hollowed skulls
that corrode on the shore, brain-washed
by robber waves that sob over them, jibing
the missed chances, the terminal illness
that spread crablike to the last paralysis.

Leave them there, but don't look backwards
to the island of broken bones.
Rise through the air with eyes gleaming
heart relit, hair sheened to the sun,
metamorphic hope on the mainland
heralding your return.

Suburban mum

Tealady

The woman in my teapot
smiles when I smile —
flaws are obvious
in stainless steel,
chromium furrows
around the eyes,
metallic cruel
duplicity of chins.

The woman in my teapot
simmers and stirs
tealeaf oracles
conjuring the future's
quicksilver alchemy:
satanic mixture
of tea and verse.
Nudging forty
cups that flow over
are seldom hers.

The woman in my teapot
wears a long face
nods when I nod
spends time reflecting
things might go better with
coke or bitters;
sipping the tannin she
tends to agree
life's a shit sandwich
when taken with tea.

Hen In A Boat

Black hen laid an egg
in our fibreglass boat
becalmed on a concrete
automobile slipway
remote from water.
(She considered it well
with her head on one side
weighing each possibility).
We said, how silly,
a hen in a boat,
what was she intending?
Perhaps she wished to float
from her present moorings
(as sometimes we do —
why else harbour boats
in suburban backyards?)
Or she felt marooned
wished concrete were water
or *air* for that matter
having tried all thirty-two
perches to sit upon
yet found herself wanting
new places for nesting
swift wings over water
horizons of birds who
could fly, who could fly.

little dippers

Among the rubble of the stars
             disfigured constellations
Ursa Major   Great Bear   whatever
and those that fail to culminate
like us   suburban mums   little dippers
milky ways   no longer luminous
meteors   off course
friction with air   burnt up
             S O M E W H E R E
an idea winks   red eyed   persistent
glows brightly   refuses stubbornly
             to settle
             for less than
horizons opening upwards

             Even for stars
there is only brief incandescence
             Light years
measure space   not brilliance
             Ideas
glow like torches in the night
             uneasily put out
Sisters   let us
             take up the light
repeat   refractions
             to
                  i
                   n
                    f
                     i
                      n
                       i
                        t
                         y

Pianola

Tonight, we were young again
Bob Slack, executive
grey-haired, fed paper rolls
to his computer-style
heirloom pianola
expertly pedalling
all those worn print-out songs
There's A Long Hapsburg *Trail*
and *An Old Spinning Wheel*
in his loud baritone
Danny, Oh Boy, The Pipes
One Day When We Were Young
Mary, embarrassed, said
wifely, the neighbours, Bob
Perfect Day, what will they think
Memory Has Painted It
Roses, our yesteryear
Blooming In Picardy
icechests and ginger beer
rich home-made poverty
misty-eyed now we sing
Hearts Of Oak, following
high on nostalgia
Bob's pianola

Growing Crystals

My son, growing crystals
in his downstairs laboratory,
toyed for weeks with granules
of quartz, felspar, mica
searching the slivered granite
along the plane of cleavage point,
tapping the rich rock core
of crystalline secrets.
At last, treading the diamond edge
of thirteen-year-old wisdom,
he raised from copper sulphate
(poisonously blue in its glass beaker)
a jewel, prismed, luminous.
Holding it a hair's length away
he thought it was miraculous
and called me to the viewing.
Atoms at work, he told me,
making things enormous.

Shades

Cabbage Tree Creek
for Frank de Silva

When they announced your death on radio
you were just another motorist
(what with the race-results from Eagle Farm
and collapse of a cricketer from England)
Francis Kenneth De Silva, Murphy Road,
hit by a semi-trailer. No mention, none,
of painter/teacher, all those canvases
of landscaped earth, little boats at Bribie,
Stanthorpe vineyards, legendary goldmines
and the rich crushed ore of Boonah sunset
lifting the Maroon Dam to sky.

And Cabbage Tree Creek, you said, was blue
that day, it really was
a Danube
with cabbagegum and scribbly paperbark
falling in with your wishes, bending over
three happy people, a family fishing?
admiring the creek, contemplative forever.

In my loungeroom gallery you sit
uneasily with Holmyard, Weber, Guy
(''I don't use photographs, won't, don't'')
compatible with Williams, Hart, Macqueen
and somehow steal the show. Lately I see
you've disciplined youth's recklessness,
the orphan's rage. This is essential art:
angry fire quenched, passion distilled —
one treeladen muddy Brisbane stream
reflecting sky, the grace in all of us.

Today the Creek moves off my cedar wall
and flows across the room. It's all right,
Frank. It's right. God, I see it all.

Toowong Cemetery

Here are the uninterred
shades of the living dead —
miles of white tombstones,
angels gilt-faced or bleached
pale ornate cherubim
measuring the hillside
with deadly precision
row upon chiselled row:
loud marble testimony
to have-beens below.

It does seem unreasonable
to advertise nonentities
with grand superstructures.
Even the Pyramids boast less.
These days, one sees
plain burials
simple crosses
hygienic cremations
minimum fuss.
Rarely tombstones.

My car tends to baulk
at those graven images
along Birdwood Terrace.
Some might have preferred
when the spirit had flown
humbly to enrich the earth
naked, without brazen stone
proclaiming their reliquaries,
with only the rain
and wind rippling the air
quietly in death.

The Plot

"Harder to get in
than out", said the sexton.
"Toowong now is closed:
the oldest and best
cemetery in Brisbane.
        This cancellation
below Governors' Hill
will hold eight people —
you have six children? —
four sites 9 by 3.
        Seven-foot deep
solid rock excavation
will cost a bit extra
but you pay for that later
after your funeral.
        Bodies keep better
in rock. You should see
old ones from loose soil.
        Because of delay
with a granite-faced burial
the holes are dug early
before you are dead;
filled in again, ready."

We stood, inspecting.
        Somewhere a bird
sang a premature blessing
upon our interment.
        Jackhammers stopped
vibrating the shale.
Our hearts kept on beating.
        An invisible man
tossed dirt with a shovel
from way down a hole.
His hat dispossessed
seemed to move on its own
below ground level.

> Quite unimpressed
at this sleight-of-head
the sexton was waiting.

"Yes", we said.
(I'd always wanted
something quite different,
a shade tree, a view —
not that it mattered).
We left a down payment
a kind of reward
for a plot where our lives
hung in the balance.
The sexton recorded
our luck. Cancellation
was rare. Himself,
he was having cremation.

Centripetal

He is whistling in my tomb already
the bird with the bloodred throat.

All of mankind gleams in the molecule
of his eye, in his gold-prismed feathers.

In the cratered silence of the moon
his sound pierces the space capsule.

He calls at motorcades, time machines
assassins of presidents,

at neutron bombs scarring the planets,
Vesuvius, Noah's Ark and Ra.

The first papyrus boats pluming the Atlantic
heard his cries out of Belsen and Hiroshima.

Even the flare of Apollo Five astronauts
burning to death, rose over Heliopolis

for all time is NOW in eternity
the past/present/future of oneness.

O bird with a four-chambered heart like mine
tune me to your immortal wavelength,

spilling your song over galaxies
into this small clay dwelling!

I who fly in diminishing circles
close my ears to your fire-tongued singing.

Becoming
to Andre Gide

Incomprehensible.
Blue eyes, staring,
lids closed by fingers.
What do you see in death
pour soi, conscious self,
life's fragile beauty
or death's trick fulfillment,
mind over matter?

Unspeakable.
The slow decay, proud flesh
falling away
from the skull's barrier.

Unthinkable. Yet I think
of your dead blue eyes
scanning infinity:
empty eyesockets
stare into the braincage
finally picked clean —
vision of Truth
and no way for weeping.
Bone upon bone, has-been,
are you now the sum
of your acts? *Devenir.*
You are not: you have become.
Devenu. Continuing self
God only knows what
is *becoming*
to you.

Death Of A Truckie

Morrie is dead. Morrie is dead.
At breakneck speed he lived, harrowed
by barbs of guilt, demon-knives of fear
sharp at the throat, cutting intentions
resolutions to shreds, always tomorrow
promising release from this day's sorrow.

Truckies have deadlines. Lifelines for the dead
interstate highways stretch, unhallowed,
paved like roads to an addictive hell
with small white tablets, signal-posts that flash
briefly through the stroboscopic night,
tired eyeballs suddenly turned bright.

A tripsheet. A weighbridge. A time
to absorb urgency into the system.
Motors rev, vibrate. Reflexes quicken.
Headlights blaze at every terminal.
Trucks crisscross frayed borders of the mind
closed to a circuit. Tarpaulins flap the wind.

Mad. Mad. A shrewd, secretive madness
lurks in the hidden bottle. Thirst craves,
splits the eyeball. Lungs burst
with air of fire. Blankfaced he raves
at wife and children, cursing the deep
pain that cries the night to sleep.

    This bed
has needles puncturing the spine:
shafts of remorse penetrate the head.
When thirst bores its hole in your liver
Amphetamine, "Speed", is the answer.

Up and away! Let there be speed
throttling the night, gobbling the miles
eighty to the hour. Roadlamps take flight
like red-eyed bats wheeling into the air . . .
Trapped in the wreck below the water's sheen
a bridge-post where his heart had been,
Morrie is dead.

Morrie is dead.
Dying he lived, and dead is still not dead
as long as dead men cry a hollow cry
from tomb to bleak perimeter of sky
for sun eclipsed. Morrie, once more
heavy trucks are trembling my door
and was it then your voice above the blast
crying out for peace, peace at last?

The Catch

And I said to the Lord, if I had to choose
between one good poem and a swag of Tailor
(cold, dark, the hook rebaited
a dozen times over, without any luck
and children protesting aloud for dinner)
or even that gift of loaves and fishes
(a netful wriggling, with bread thrown in)
I'd take the poem. Just then he struck,
a whopping Jew. We ate well that night.

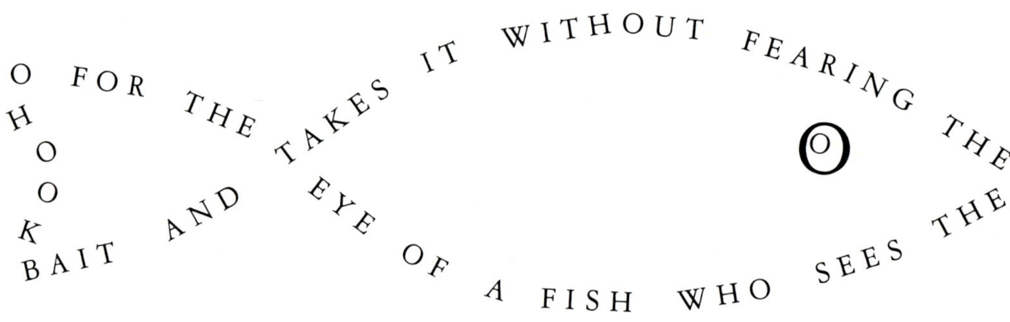

FISH

I

FINISH